Selected Poems

John Wieners

Jonathan Cape Thirty Bedford Square London

First published 1972
© 1972 by John Wieners

Jonathan Cape Ltd, 30 Bedford Square, London WC1

ISBN 0 224 61572 6

Poems have been taken from the following: *The Hotel
Wentley Poems* (Auerhahn Press, San Francisco),
© 1958 by John Wieners; *Ace of Pentacles* (James F.
Carr & Robert A. Wilson, New York), © 1964 by
John Wieners; *Pressed Wafer* (The Gallery Upstairs
Press, Buffalo), © 1967 by John Wieners; *Asylum
Poems* (Angel Hair Books, New York), © 1969 by
John Wieners; *Nerves* (Cape Goliard Press, London), © 1970
by John Wieners

Printed and bound in Great Britain
by Richard Clay (The Chaucer Press), Ltd
Bungay, Suffolk

Preface

Verse making is more than a continuum of principle resting on feminine phenomenological apprehension. The real one of many, the illusory far and near intersect to push behaviour's stream, dependent on questing, producing revelatory postures for men, animals and stars.

The poet is one pastor of this distribution between two visions.

Illusory form heightened by denial arises from contraction of desire, stilling propagation. To stay with one's self requires position and perhaps provision, realizing quality out of strangeness.

The quality of gift being alone.

Wraiths cross time.

The gift of quality seems rather removed from processes practiced today over the counter, behind the bar and desk in lobbies of service. Interferences from gifts hamper realization, but they may be used as reinforcement of sensory apparatus. Proximate distractions show little more than confusion and to promulgate them as verse scatters ultimate sights, the true brothered quality of what we condense and what to allow constant.

The permanent evident search for labour and trial makes dignity trivial. Visual order obeys gravity, but genuine shimmering substance cognates more than complacencies of constant worth. It holds radiation, that force attracts, draws and breathes.

An indoctrination to quality could be a return to places of origin, one instance of namely objects, the second an absolute rendition of balance and movement, the third transformations by fire, the easiest of all, if will be inherited. To true the present gleams more than conditions of peseudo-morphology, it asks one submit to discipline's enduring form.

Contents

Selected Poems

Scenes for a Film

The poet in perpetual torment:
He enters a telephone booth. Light from neon overhead outside the booth illumines only his face. He wears a tan trenchcoat, with the collar pulled up about his chin. He dials once, hangs up, his thin hands tremble as he dials again, waits for the face to spell out the number of letters in 'I love you', then hangs up; his hands shake as he dials again, palsy the line is busy, his cigarette drops as he rings the fourth time.

He is afraid the sound of his heart will break glass in the booth, he waits: a voice at the other end of the line says: Hello ... hello ... the poet sees the old room with a face and its mouth pressed against the telephone's mouth ... the poet's eyes close, 'Just once more.' He hears the hello, then click. The poet comes out, a smile as after sex is on his face.

He walks a wide street. A man in elegant dinner clothes passes by among others. He has a handkerchief to his face, he removes it for the poet to see blood on the right and left side of his forehead and on his nose, crimson against his Florida tan. It is Reb Barker. No one else sees. The poet keeps on looking as the man staggers against an iron chain drawn to close an empty parking lot. The poet turns from the wide street onto another lane going steeply uphill, one side lined with American automobiles dotted under street lamps. He steps across the walk from a lit façade five stories up. He watches a thick shadow move against the light. There are no shades, only white curtains. He sees no one inside except silhouettes. He enters a doorway so as not to be seen. There are four windows and a pair of hands open one, then the curtains flutter and all lights go out at once, the curtains drop lower and lower across the street, gentle in the wind until they blow across the poet's face. He touches their hem, admiring his hand through the gauze, then brushes the fabric aside, so that they hang short against the tenement wall. He continues walking the steep hill under the lamps, very heavy his feet, one after another, past a thick mailbox, until he reaches the top where he looks down the bottom to strain and see the curtains again, but cannot as he turns onto a narrow straight alley, lined with overhanging houses. No one is out. He passes an old hotel: with words painted in black on a marble desk in the lobby: CHAMBERS FOR MEN. He continues on. There is no one in the lobby.

He comes to a house on the corner of a grey square, most spacious and lined with what appears to be the back of a Grecian temple, whose pillars do not begin on the ground, they start at the top of a wall, twenty feet high. The wall has doors in it, they are barred.

He places a tin key in the front latch of the house opposite the temple. The portiere has smoked glass panels. The key only goes half-in, when he turns it, it bends there, he turns it back slowly and pushes in. His face has the same look as in the telephone booth, and suddenly it is very warm. He sweats. It must be summer. He hits it with his palm and it slowly goes in a knotch. With his fist. It is all the way in. He pushes open the door to a small semi-circular lobby with mirrors clouded from age.

He sees himself in full view, with red and white striped jersey and blue cord trousers. He is barefoot. There is one floor lamp on an old shade. Light falls to the floor, making shadows under his chin, his cheekbones black and his eyes deep. The entrance hall is tall and there are white closed doors to the left and right. They are bolted. He looks up, begins to climb. A wide stairway circles around and around six flights, its creaking bannisters showing way to the top. He reaches the first landing, where a bare bulb hangs. There is a window with a filthy torn green shade hanging from a cornice. He passes under the small lamp, turns to climb again. On the second floor, a boarded alcove shows the only glimmer of light. He pushes open the handle into a marble lavatory, again borrowing a bare bulb to save one from total darkness. The walls are pink, but crawling with roaches.

In the middle of the wall, beside a marble basin is again another door, this too swollen from heat. Behind, a room with three windows at its end, looking down onto the temple square. Street shadows come from outside, as he goes into the inner room. Windows are shut and hung again with white transparent curtains. On one side of the chamber, an ivory marble fireplace blocked and streaked with yellow bends luminously in the heat. Hanging off the Victorian ceiling, a chandelier with a light socket from its heart has twin cords swinging over to an outsize lamp beside a mammoth wrought-iron bed, filling half the sanctuary with appliances, the connections so huge they stretch from the sitting room's center to a wrought-metal table reaching halfway up the wall.

There are two men asleep in bed with a white sheet pulled up to their naked chests. There is room for him on the outside. They are on their backs. He removes his red shirt and trousers and goes to bed noisily, hoping they will wake up. He waits. They remain as they were ... One snores and the other says, Turn over on your back, Basil, for god's sake. The poet looks at his arms outside the sheet. The light cord drops over the bed in a deep swoop, hanging from the socket in what appears to be a noose to his slowly closing eyes.

The Windows

Delaunay wrote on the back of his painting, Simultaneous Windows:
'This document had to be returned to a poet.' And he gave it to one,
Jean Cassou. When Apollinaire likewise saw the painting, he wrote
Les Fenêtres. Now how do I come to The Windows? They open by
themselves and I look out of them for my own view, see each color
in his painting as a place, each line in his poem as a *poem*, entire to
itself, a sound and end in itself, without periods. There are no connections. Yet, look how each of us is hooked.

From red to green all the yellow runs
When they sing Arise in the national forest
A bat is pinned to a tree
This is a poem for birds with only one wing
We cannot take calls by telephone
Terror is a giant
It is the color of your eyes
See how our lady plays all day with those dead Tunisians
The poor young man munches on his own white tie
You sit a naked cool rider
Now watch the windows open by themselves
Arranged with tissue paper hands of light
Beauté paler than manila violets
We transplant in vain what cannot blossom
Old lady Lotte keeps time by sundials but her Shadow
    knows the score
An old pair of yellow slippers before the window
Towers
Towers crumble to the street
Pits open up everywhere
Southern trees bear strange crêpe to bury vagabonds
In shoeboxes painted forlorn
While reeds whine through trumpets up north
Where strippers off stage
Sell their skin cheap as ice
Tinkling like diamonds

Vancouver
The train full of negroes and snow balls all winter

O Paris
From red to green all the yellow runs
Paris Vancouver Hyannis Avignon New York
    and Antilles
This window opens itself as an orange
Bowl of fruit full of light

San Francisco

night
clubs. The band (all black) starts at six
       A M to swing. A—
       round nine, big Eric on guitar
strings
blue, B girls at bar
       sit hair bleached
silver
white.
'I don't know no
body, and nobody knows me,

my husband's best friend
      comes
      up behind me
         Wham.
I try to be broad-
minded you know for twenty years,
there was only one race for me
         this black
bastard, my ex-
husband's best
friend that 's the last captain
       midnight to cross this channel.'

Drapes
to the door, Al
   with Rocky tends bar : get that sun
        out of here, in
comes a new platinum baby :
          O.K. baby, and how are you?
   Drunk.
   Swinging her green parasol.

   Dancing Irene lost her
slippers, black slacks droop, and gimp

glides a swan just
her and colored cat all over the floor.

                                     Everyone knows
       she is the key to open
your golden store
     gets us a cab even to ride
                         home in with
                         out a red cent.
Our eyeballs are cool, I say Look, man
                     it's the sun!

'Peyote' poem

With no fresh air in my lungs
                    in the middle of
the night, inhabited by strange gods
                                    who
are they, they walk by in white trenchcoats
    with pkgs. of paradise in their pockets.

Their hands.

from *The Hotel Wentley Poems*
A poem for record players

The scene changes

Five hours later
I come into a room
where a clock ticks.
I find a pillow to
muffle sounds I make,
engaged in taking away
from God his sound,
the pigeons somewhere
above me, the cough
a man makes down the hall,
the flap of wings
below me, squeak
of sparrows in the alley,
            landing
            under the bay
window out my window.
All dull details
I only describe
but which are here
I hear and shall never
give up again, shall carry
with me over streets
of this seacoast city,
forever, oh clack your
metal wings god, you are
mine now in the morning.
I have you by the ears
in exhaust pipes of
a thousand cars gunning
their motors turning over
all over town.
            6.15.58.

A poem for painters

Our age bereft of nobility
How may our faces show it?
I look for love.
My lips stand out
dry and cracked with want
of it.
Oh it is well.
My poem shall show the need for it.

Again we go driven by forces
we have no control over. Only
in the poem
comes an image that we rule
the line by the pen
in the painter's hand one foot
away from me.

Drawing the face
and its torture.
That is why no one dares tackle it.
Held as they are in hands
of forces they
cannot understand.
That despair
is on my face and shall show
in the fine lines of any man.

I held love once in the palm of my hand.
See the lines there.
How we played
its game, are playing now
in bounds of white and heartless fields.
Fall down on my head, love
drench my flesh in streams
of fine sprays. Like

                    French perfume
so I light up as
                    mountain glorys
and am showered by scent
          of the finished line.
                    No circles

          but that two parallels do cross
and carry our souls and bodies
     together as planets,
               showing light on the surface
                    of our skin, knowing
                         so much flows through
                    the veins underneath
               our cheeks puffed with it,
                    the pockets full.

2.

Pushed on by incompletion
          of what goes before me
I hesitate before this paper
          scratching for right words.

Paul Klee scratched for seven years
          on smoked glass, to develop
          his line, LaVigne says, look
at his face! he who has spent
          all night drawing mine.

          The sun also
rises on the rooftops, beginning
w/ violet. I begin in blue
knowing why we are cool.

3.

My middle name is Joseph and I
walk beside an ass on the way to what
Bethlehem, where a new babe is born.

Not the second hand of Yeats but
first prints on a cloudy windowpane.

America, you boil over

4.

        The cauldron scalds.
        Flesh is scarred.
        Eyes shot.

        Streets aswarm with
        vipers and heavy armed bandits.
        There are bandages on wounds
        but blood flows unabated. The bath-
        rooms are full. Oh stop up
                        the drains.
            We are run over.

5.

Let me ramble here.
Yet stay within my own yardlines.
I go out of bounds
        without defense
or attack.

6.

        The last game is over
        The line lengthens
Let us stay with what we know.
Love is my strength,
overpowered by
            desire, that too
on the face's gone stale.
When green was the bed my love
and I laid down upon.
Such it is, heart's complaint,

you hear upon a day in June.
And I see no end in view
when summer goes, as it will
upon the roads, like singing
companions across the land.

Go with it man, if you must,
but leave us markers on your way,

South of Mission, Seattle,
over the Sierra Mountains,
the Middle West and Michigan,
moving east again, easy
coming into Chicago and
cattle country, calling
to each other over canyons,
careful not to be caught
at night, they are still out,
the destroyers, and down
into the South, familiar land,
lush places, blue mountains
of Carolina, into Black Mountain
and you may sleep out, or
straight across into States

I cannot think of their names.

This nation is so large, like
our hands, our love it lives
with no lover, looking only
for the beloved, back home
into the heart, New York,
New England, Vermont green
mountains, and Massachusetts
my city, Boston and the sea.
Again to smell what this calm
ocean cannot tell us. The seasons.
Only the heart remembers
and records in words
of those works

we lay down for what men
can come to them.

7.

At last. I come to the last defense.

My poems contain no
            wilde beestes, no
lady of the lake music
of the spheres, or organ chants,

yet by these lines
I betray what little given me.

One needs no defense.

        Only the score of a man's
        struggle to stay with
        what is his own, what
        lies within him to do.

        Without which is nothing,
        for him or those who hear him
        and I come to this,
        knowing the waste, leaving

        the rest up to love
        and its twisted faces
        my hands claw out at
        only to draw back from the
        blood already running there.

        Oh come back, whatever heart
        you have left. It is my life
        you save. The poem is done.
                        6. 18. 58.

A poem for early risers

1.

I'm infused with the day
even
tho
the
day
may
destroy
me

I'm out in it
Placating
it.
Saving
myself

from demons
who sit in blue
coats, carping
at us across
tables. Oh they
go out the doors.
I am done with
them. I am
done with faces
I have seen before.

For me now the new.
Unturned tricks
of the trade : the Place
of the heart where man
is afraid to go.

It is not doors. It is
the ground of my soul

where dinosaurs left
their marks. Their tracks
are upon me. They
walk flatfooted.
Leave heavy heels and
turn sour green
fields where I eat with
ease. Good to
throw them up, good
to hear my stomach growl.
After all, I am possessed
by wild animals and
long haired men
women who gallop
breaking over my beloved
places. Oh put down
thy vanity man the
old man told us under
the tent. You are over-
run with ants.

2.

Man lines up for his
breakfast in the dawn
unaware of the jungle
left behind
in his sleep. Where
fields flourished
with cacti, cauliflower
all the uneatable foods
that morning man
perishes, if he remembered.

3.

And yet we must remember
The old forest, wild

screams in the backyard
or cries in the bedroom.
It is ours to nourish.
The nature to nurture.
Dark places where
woman holds, hands
us herself, handles an
orange ball. Throwing it
up for spring. Like
the clot/my grandfather
vomited/months before
he died of cancer. And
spoke of later in terror.

6. 20. 58.

A poem for cocksuckers

Well we can go
in the queer bars w/
our long hair reaching
down to the ground and
we may sing our songs
of love like the black mama
on the juke box, after all
what have we got left.

    On our right the fairies
giggle in their lacquered
voices & blow
smoke in your eyes let them
it's a nigger's world.
The gifts do not desert us,
fountains do not dry
up there are rivers running,
mountains
swelling for spring to cascade.
    It is all here between
      powdered legs &
painted eyes of the fairy
friends who do not fail us
      in our hour of
      despair. Take not
away from me the small fires
I burn in memory of love.

                6. 20. 58.

A poem for the old man

God love you
   Dana my lover
lost in the horde on
this Friday night,
500 men are moving up
& down from the bath
room to the bar.
Remove this desire
from the man I love.
Who has opened
   the savagery
of the sea to me.

See to it
his wants are filled
on California Street.
Bestow on him lar-
gesse that allows him
peace in his loins.

Leave him not
to the moths.
Make him out a lion
so that all who see him
hero worship his
thick chest as I did
moving my mouth
over his back bringing
our hearts to heights
I never hike over
   anymore.

Let blond hair burn
on the back of his
neck, let no ache

screw his face
up in pain, his soul
   is so hooked.
Not heroin.
Rather fix these
hundred men as his
lovers & lift him
with the enormous bale
of their desire.

                    6. 20. 58.

A poem for museum goers

I walk down a long
passage way with a
red door waiting open.

It is Edvard Munch.
Turn right, turn
I see my sister

hanging beside the wall,
heavy breasts and hair
tied to a tree in the garden

with full moon
are ladies of the street.
Whipped for whoring.

Their long hair binds them.

They have lain long
hours in bed, blood
on their mouths, arms
reaching down for
ground not given them.

They are enveloped
in pain. Bah.
There is none. Munch

knew it. Put the
Shriek in their ears
to remove it from his own.
Open thy mouth, tell us
from what landscape you
have escaped,
            Fishing
boats are in the bay, no

c

outgoing tides for you
whom he anchored to
                        Hell.

Even here young lovers
cast black shadows.
Nets are down.

Huge seasnakes
squirm on shore
taking away even
the beach from us.

Move on. Moonlight

I see the garden women
in their gravy days
when hair hung golden or

black to the
floor & the walls
were velvet.

An old sailor his face like wood
his chin splintered
by many shipwrecks
keeps their story
in his eyes. How the house
at the top of the drive
held them all, their lovers,

with Munch the most
obsessed. His face
carved by knife blades.

Lover leaves lover,
1896, 62 years
later, the men
sit, paws and
jagged depths
under their heads,

now the season of
the furnished room. Gone
the Grecian walls & the

cypress trees,
plain planks, spider
webs, a bed

only big enough for one,
it looks like a
casket. Death

death on every
wall, guillotined
and streaming in
flames.

6. 21.58.

A poem for the insane

The 2nd afternoon I come
back to women of Munch.

Models with god over
their shoulders, vampires,

the heads are down and
blood is the water-
                  color
they use to turn on.

Their story is not done.
There is one wall
left to walk. Yeah—

Afterwards—Nathan
gone, Big Eric busted,
Swanson down. It is

right, the Melancholy
on the Beach. I do not
                 split
but hang onto the demon

Tree, while shadows drift
around me. Until at last
there is left only

the Death Chamber. Family Reunion
in it. Rocking chairs and
who is the young man

who sneaks out thru
the black curtain away
from the bad bed.

Yeah stand now
on the new road, with
the huge mountain on your

right out of the mist, the
Bridge before me,
the woman waiting

with no mouth, waiting
for me to kiss it on.
I will. I will walk with

my eyes up on you for
ever. We step into
the Kiss, 1897.

Light streams.
Melancholy carries
a red sky and our dreams

are blue boats
no one can bust or
blow out to sea.

We ride them
and Tingel-Tangel
in the afternoon.

6. 23. 58.

finis

238 Cambridge Street
An Occasional verse

We're back on the scene
again with linoleum floors
and Billie H blowing the blues
fine & mellow it is with PG
cooking in the kitchen,
Jennifer walking through the rooms
'What are you talking about
you know you're gonna get some,'—
she says to Melly but
it ain't the same, baby,
her old man's in Mexico and
mine, mine's a square in
San Francisco while we
haunt an old city on the Atlantic
waiting in the night for a fix.

January 6th Nativity 1959

As Preface to *Transmutations*

How long ago Steve it was
we walked along Arlington Street
throwing words to wind
before junk, before jail before
we moved to 4 corners
          of the world.
You lived on Grove Street
and wrote poems poems poems
to the Navy, to Marshall, to Boston
Common. A simple life.
          Frantic comedown.
I look now out a backyard in
          San Francisco,
Easter Sunday organ music
thru the room below,
          gone our lovers
gone Arlington, Beacon and Charles
          Streets, March 29
1959, 6 months in Danvers.
          How can the poem
show in your eyes in those dark cells?
Bang. Arlington Street comes down
          with a clump.
Oh for a blade of grass. Oh for a room
          with the rent paid.
Oh for a roof.
          I see before me the cobblestones
and camera. Dana and you
          in the sun ducking
out of the lens.
          You cannot move
faster than the shutter of my mind.

          Elms bend over
the street and form an arch

                    we walk under,
sad priests in the 20th century.
                    We began the second half
together, chalked our words
                    on red brick
and left them for the rain.
                    It is not kind.
Nor time. Nor memory the Mother,
                    a thing of barbs and
needles. The street is long.
                    It runs to ends
                    of the earth.
                    We are still
                    on it.
                    But cannot see
or hear the other.
                    What traffic
                    drowns out
                    all our notes.
                          1959.

Act 2

I took love home with me,
we fixed in the night to
sink into a stinging flash.

¼ grain of love
        we had,
2 men on a cot, silk
cover and green cloth
over the lamp,
        the music was just right.
I blew him like a symphony.
    It floated and
        he took me
down the street to
        leave me here.
3 AM. No sign.

        only a moving van
        up Van Ness Avenue.

Foster's never like this.

I'll walk home, up the
        same hills we
            came down.
He'll never come back,
        there'll be no horse
            tomorrow nor pot
tonight to smoke till dawn.

He's gone and taken
my morphine with him
Oh Johnny. Women in
    the night moan yr. name
                    6.19.59.

Larkspur

then swing to Topsy, cool bass
behind the waves of
easy living
when you're in love
building up scales
like a roof
out of leaves and grass, taking a breath
on a reed your
end just right
And nowhere in sight,
he says
expecting it to come down
any second.
My boat
from the sky

In love

A simple song
to long for home and him
lounging there under the moon.
What is he? Who is my heart
he should mean this much to me?

Is it sex, or grass stains on your shirt?
night, or sight of flesh
lying on its side in the Pine Grove?

Groove of memory, overgrown with weed
                    and speedballs,
barren trees, or summer garden,
hate and blood, or flood of seed
                    from ardent partner?

Who can say, what declares care
demands desire
for his hands through your hair,
the sudden flight of birds
that brings him home despite dim stars.

At Big Sur

Lizard under stone,
bees buzz around us
through two trees full of canaries
and in burnt grass
yellow poppies.

Louise

Wind shakes a guitar in the house tonight
a dog barks just once
at the non-existent moon

A maiden strums alone in golden light
lovers say goodbye without words
their eyes to the rising sun

Wrapped up in an Indian blanket

mist miles out
on the Pacific
fog blocks up view.

W. Cather's book
from The Stone House
on Big Sur in

California. Book of
prairies, book of love
poems to Spanish Johnny

(what a rush
when we write his name.
'On a silver cup bought in Venice'

life is sweet together.
Birds in branches,
these broken lines

writing under a roof
open to sky
writing on stone.

Woman of prairies
waiting for his face
to rise on cliffs of the moon.

San Francisco, 1958

And always these tropical songs call me forth
            into south, lush land
        denied long time now, its
                heat and speed embraced
                    in yellow flares'
                        solo flight.
Breasts of Mexico sybillant against
        ear, a rose along flesh
                in pharmacia with
                    spikes and needles.
Pin Vera Cruz. Prefix dans Mexicali
            by Nemi or Bop. Ah Cinerama!
A red horn strokes sky. Cheap
                visions of highway
                motels. Move over
                guitar strums. Storms flush
        Camino Real at top of eye-
                lids, this is the place
baby he said where everyone comes to
                    ball
            on a tin can joint

Pool of Light

a shimmering fern leaf, 2 upraised em-
    blems of gold
      lift instant trem-
        blings revolved.

O Switzerland, O Schön castle, a land across Rhine.

Windows of Waltham

Sol, *Bronze Age came first* Sol,
   Wong, before snow nothing came.
Don't worry about the wisdom of
                               the past.
Two met and made a first.

Acts of Youth

I

With great fear I inhabit the middle of night
What wrecks of mind await, what drugs
to dull the senses, what little there is left,
what more may be taken away?

Fear of travelling, future without hope
or buoy. I must get away from this place and see
there is no fear without me: only within
unless it be some sudden act or calamity

to land me in the hospital again, a total wreck
without memory, or worse still, behind bars.
If one could just get out of the country. Some place
where he may eat the lotus in peace.

For in this country it is terror, poverty awaits; or
am I a marked man, my life a lesson
or experience to those young who would trod
the same path, without God

unless he be one of justice, to wreak vengeance
on acts committed while young under un-
due influence or circumstance. Oh I have always
seen my life as drama, patterned after

those who met with disaster or doom.
Is my mind being taken away me.
I have been over the abyss before. What
is that ringing in my ears that tells

me all is nigh, is naught but roaring of the winter wind.
Woe to those homeless out on this night.
Woe to those crimes committed from which we
may walk away unharmed.

2.

So turn on the light
Smoke rings rise in the air.
Do not think of the future; there is none
but the formula all great art is made from

pain and suffering. Give one strength
to bear it, to enter those places where
the great animals are caged. And we may live
at peace by their side. A bride to no burden

god imposes but knows we have the means
to sustain its force unto the end of our days.
For that it is what we are made for; for that
we are created. Until the dark hours are done.

And we rise again at dawn.
Infinite particles of the divine sun, now
worshipped in pitches of the night.

from *The Joyous Cosmology*

For I have seen love and
his face is choice Heart of Hearts,
a flesh of pure fire, fusing from the center
where all Motion are one.

And I have known
despair this face has ceased to stare
at me with the Rose of the world
but lies furled

in an artificial paradise it is Hell to get into.
If I knew you were there
I would fall upon my knees and plead God
to deliver you in my arms once again.

But it is senseless to try.
One can only take means to reduce misery
confuse the sensations, so that this Face,
what aches in the heart and makes each new

start less close to the source of desire,
fade from the flesh that fires the Night
with dreams and unutterable longing.

Tuesday 7:00 PM

There is majesty in rose light
across the sky
at twilight on Tuesday
afternoon.

When November night
comes up from Central Park
to surround empire towers
around the dark

trees wave
in cold breeze.
And I am lost beside
the furs and homburgs

on Fifth and Fifty-Seventh Sts.
when Black Starr and Frost
holds its annual sale
of diamonds,

precious stones aloft
in zones of heaven.
Haven of the heart
this is that new start

long at last awaited—
journey to the stars, who stay
at the Chatham, Gotham and Pierre.

They stare from block of walled-in gardens
to penthouses, where with glare of yesteryear
hard-eyed maidens scan the air

for slope of easy gentlemen there.
Gowns trail across cobblestones.
Homes are lit by fires in the grate.

Cased on windows hang the hopes
of the poor in damask silk.
Yet blue for the touch of your hand

who could lead me to the grand ballroom
and library bookcases eased in oak,
my dreams are there and pledged to

be fulfilled as they go up in smoke.

The Serpent's Hiss

Cold comes creeping in window
And in sky searchlights sweep
  countryside
O frozen loneliness that does not thaw
Nor let me sleep.

I count moments until dawn
And suppress stars that wheel in deep

Ocean of space, where we at length will lie
Until our dust mingles with fathom
   less abyss
Of time; all air ours to fly
Amid rose petals of some forgotten
   hand

That flowers in the night like moon.

153 Avenue C

The night cold
I lie abed,
drugged.

The gas heater on.
I would it were
Off

To snuff out my life.

Ancient blue star!

seen out the car
window.
One blinking light
how many miles away
stirs in mind
a human condition

When paved alone
created of lust
we wrestle with stone
for answer to dust.

Mermaid's Song

If thou in me the full flush of love see
Know it comes from the rose that magnifies
To breathe in some corner of that sure sky,
A coarser blossom than eternity
Likewise perishing and lost from earth
To bloom anew in realms beyond pain
Where fleshly vision cruel time disdain.

If this be said I loved with all my worth
Then with thee gone hold thee closer still
Than if thy cheek pressed up against my hand
And will go on loving thee sweet until
My name and thine past erased from sand
For that substance contrary to belief
Rocks eternal as an ocean's grief.

Anniversary

He too must with me wash his body, though
at far distant time, over endless space
take the cloth unto his loins, upon his face
engage in the self same *toilet* as I do now.

Cigarette between his lips, would they were mine
by this present moon swear allegiance
if he ever look, see clouds and beaches
in the sky, by stars lend his eyes shine.

What care I for miles, rows of friends lined
up in groups, blue songs, day's bright glare.
Once he was there, now gone searched empty air
this candle feeds on, find eyes, my heart's blind

to love and all he was capable of, sweet patience
when he put his lips to places I cannot name
because changed, now not the same
sun shines sad larks break forth
from winter branches.

Waste

Poetry a noble art, it
comes from well born sons.
Futile for me to start
As to see a midnight sun.

What landscape of the heart
May I set pattern to?
Arteries, pulmonary chart
Or where veins run blue?

I know the vessels' cart
Stained gold, black velvet hung
But of its richer part
Know none.

L'Impératrice

who sits supreme above all human ecstasy.
        Nine star circle of dominion about
           her head
             crown of heaven atop it.
        Who falls not, but smoke
incense to her eyes, our acts held in claws
        of falcon at her right hand.
Sceptre and pole, cross and globe to her left.

        Lily growing out of hip,
        half moon crushed to quarter
             under bare foot
        Lady of the blue robe

Scent of sperm, cloud of devotion to her nostrils.
           And pale
        wings of heaven behind
             her back.
        Difficult image hazy for the mind
          out of focus,
this description inadequate
        to the infinity inherent in her
        patience sitting on a throne
          or pillared seat.

        Through the ages, number 3
         girdled in gold

          with objects of eternity
           about her, and
            on display
        for our eyes worn out with love.

Deepsea

5.8

Dirt under my nails,
my hands hardcaked with
abuses of lust, despair
and drugs.

Night a foreign place,
without sound or shadow
we lie abed awaiting pills
to take effect.

No poems or romance
left, only churning
without image, bereft
soft syllable denied us.

We reach, grasp for the word
as life-preserver
to sink and bob
in burning waves.

Walls alive with pictures,
faces haunt the dark. Nothing to do
but go on led by flickering of a
flame I cannot name

Pat

5.9

A small song in willows
amid words still shadows of the night,
broken birch by river
where irises, rows of light,
shine as stars across meadows
to break on dawn.
Dread night is gone,
you see suspended in a bar against the blackness
your mighty lord, who makes his way
Love in his eyes as a bride might say
to put away all fear.

Lost bride

5.22

Full moon, shine over
take cover for a lover.

Fulfil him
as the sea

fulfils its shore,
ask no more

but that the heart
be given a resting place

and at last I lay
my face against your face.

'Shall Idleness Ring Then Your Eyes Like The Pest?'—W. H. Auden

Beware that breed of men who would eat you
out of house and home; that other breed
of flesh and spirit, who accept friendship
then turn it into lechery, parasitism, leprosy.

To see you at work and take that as their sign
for pleasure, who share your pillow to steal
your half : oh this is no good : this generosity
of heart merely flame flickering on a windowsill.

'I am ill and still no peace.'
At night, they take away the moon.
With dawn the sun. Covered over by
hand of man is dung from human hearts.

Paul

It's nice under your hands
a stranger whom I've never met
before tonight but twice

It's nice beside you on the bed
where my heart bled for love.
It's nice to have you here

and having said that, dear
nice to feel your hands upon my hair
and nicer still, to know we will

meet again, start off where
your girl friend, mistress, what ever

she is, that sleeping bride
will not be on your other side.

For Jan

The girl hustles her islands of pure flesh.
There is no way to redeem her loss but words
Where ecstasy awaits at the fringe of our lips.

There in the night she sells her body to old China
For dreams all men carry in their loins.
Offend not ancestral gods, by this sale

Of love, or tasting of unknown secret pleasures
Always been our due; to inhabit at river bank
The depth of ocean in mid-stream.

Monday Sunrise

Red glow over China,
a color advertising
unable to duplicate

king's crown
burnished in chambers of North

seen over chimneys
on East River,

orange, yellow, tangerine

casts a mottled sheen
as of colour Renaissance, no
more Byzantine

Liquid
copper, bronze
topaz

      A scow sails into it,
       transformed from coal black
to Phoenician fishing boat
or submarine
raised in Yangtze

      shadows from the sea

turns a gown of
brocade or damask, a bracelet or heavy cross
of burning flame laid down upon the blue

its seething effervescence
become a poinard

stretching across banks
from Jersey to New York.

Not to mention the white
circle become a miracle upon it

                              as Renoir knew
this gold, I think in hair
of yellow girls.

The Magic of This Summer
June 23, 1963

The nights belong to us. They lie dreaming outside our
windows, curled in the sun, there on the firescape. The nights lie
dreaming outside us.

One does surely belong to Art. There do lie within us
frontiers of art, assuming shape. Form does belong to some
content. There is madness on my mind, assuming shape.
Form to be given, declared at any moment by
what lies outside, and within us. Some how or other, the
moment declares, us outside form to be given, declared
by shape, assuming us, our shape, forms remain
entirely given.
Let the truth of this moment last as long as my life
remains to be continually given, remains every moment,
to be given. The form declares
shape, given, of any, this moment, everything
declares itself in the moment, hidden itself in the declaration
of life, this moment, remains entirely given.

I sent a Post Card from Kansas City, Missouri
asking for money when I got to Washington D.C.
to Freude Mittleman, San Francisco,
    Signed my grandfather's name
     John Laffan
     No Address Given

Is there anything in fragments of life, unrealized moments
that come on us, riding along Blue Hill Parkway, beyond
the sunset, the moment of our life, come on, given over
completely to the past, given over our life, entirely
given, at any moment. This moment to be realized, shortly.

This means, you are to be given, at any moment,
the fragments of past life.

A knock sounds on the door, it destroys the sense
of well being, entirely, in the house. If there is well being
entirely in the house. I am sensed with the sound of being
familiar, over this content, the house to be inhabited by
strangers.

It seems there is nothing, entirely given over to any
moment, the bird does go along, on the firescape, the
whole process, birds descend in sunlight.

Wings ascend the air. Nature displays a lovely
shape, in the twittering trees one tries to escape.

The hand of the maker carves everything to be, come
everything, to thy own shape.

For its own being, will come our shape. Form declares
itself.

In the given moment

In every living being.

What is there to declare at any given moment,
of the form of our lives, what is there to be declared any more,
that the sun shines, there is nothing o no more lost, everything
given over in a moment, o lost and surrendered, my
castle in the sand, on the beach, o the castles surrendered,
in my air.

What is there to impose on
My life is not over. There is more to be given.
   How may I say this? There is no sense of any danger;
still my life, by
back life given many more days.

God bless them, give over to them, entirely,
the sense of new consciousness you now certainly
possess.

Roll out many more days, impose on us, the sense of
being, our life more important than many beings may
possess, forgive us our punctuation; and spheres many
now possess may be invoked, to possess our senses.

Our new orders are; cannot be any more than there
are no more many new lives to be possessed.
A sense preserved of the past moment, a new life

The sense of continuity entirely destroyed by many
new senses, continually destroyed by many new
shapes o continually destroyed, o many new spheres,
many life entirely destroyed, continued by
many spheres, entirely lost, o continually destroyed
many lost by more o continually new generation.

There is no message more shapely than this
Who am I but a mouthpiece. There is no more
shapely kingdom than this to come. O my lost again
continually, o my spheres.

You possess entirely, o destroyer of my senses,
many strange and new things O possessor of

II.

How is the sentence to be ended?

As I write now, questions of form asked
how is mind-time taken? to be asked many questions
given the mind time enough to spare

                                        time earned enough
                                              to learn
            There is time enough to ask many questions.

        Not enough time. Any new life entirely lost, o my generation
to come   O new generation, to come and be asked: Why?
            Art is a question.

You cannot be lost, or entirely destroyed—there is
no generation to come, asked as you who are left are
continually asked; o how do you come by?   And
why?   There are no further any more to be asked,
entirely one question;   what is there to make; what
more is there to ask?

What more is there to come many more asked; the question
                                        to come?
What more is there to come? is there any more, questions to
be asking?   o come;   there are many new questions to
ask;   there?   o how are the stars?

                    Is there life on any planet? O many
new stars continually fall and entirely destroyed, are
there any to come

Submit to many questions : Ask and it shall be asked
of them also. You are entirely alone and lost, new and
alone, lost. Shape then too takes place. Are there any
new forms.

I hear the sound of rushing waters.

I see planets drifting in great blobs, through immense
spaces

I don't want to see any more of this world. I close
my eyes;   blue light!

These are associations, mental images, that do not
ever exist. The mind composes itself entirely of
images, that completely study the mind's way, even
tho words written out picture only the mind's flashes

The mind, entirely composed of images creates a
form, to be flowed through blood by many particles,
entirely composed and transmitted this by many ways,
to their life.

The mind, entirely composed of images, creates
a poem. There are no different than we are.

There are no different spheres than yours

I heard a cat cry in my arm, assuming the shape
of blood Cry aloud, in my arms.

o God help me o remind my spheres to protect me,
remind me of my own spheres,

as song spins out a melody
that the mood earns

spare there moments of my own past life;
to come, o be remembered

4 : 10

Now back to our continual reality, expressed in the afternoon
window. O reality, expressed in the past life, revive these
dying senses, o wonder at again! other window curtains
blow in the sun.

Now it can be done. The sun shines again in the window.
The heat radiates a light often heavenly; light more
in the window than any where else again.   The heat
often radiates a more long life. Dying heat. More.

O let me be :   rise,
shining again
off rooftops again. o let me be, rise off again
swimmers on the rooftops.
The heat often radiates
a lovely long life.
O let me be, rise shining again
off the rooftops, swimmers in the after noon glow
of trees dry in the sun.
O let me be, rise again

o roofs hover in the trees; the lovers lie themselves
in the sun :   o rise again;   o heat radiate; o left life
long and lovely, themselves, rise shining the afternoon
light.

Sickness

I know now heard speak in the night
voices of dead loves past,

whispered instructions over electric air
confined or chained.

Down deep the path's final entrance reveals itself
in will drawn strong on palm of hand.

Do not tamper with the message there.

Do not let silent, secret reaches of the heart
                    invade you here
kept at bay long enough but he is
gone who would protect you from them.

I thought I heard voices in the courtyard
Speaking out
But it was nothing, only wind

Rattling
In a backroom of the city
under an electric light
bulb, naked.

Night's angels descend on us, it's
light become accustomed to our eyes.

Cool wind blows in open window,
I am happy being alone.
It seems time going down an eternal staircase
wound up at ease with me.

I want only the mystery of your arms around me.
Dont worry about eating my food.

Single strand of light falling on his bare shoulder
In the closet.

Won't you come and see me again,
please?

The dragon lies on its side.

For Huncke

Knowing no other god than this:
the man who places on your mouth
a kiss. Keep no mystery
but his who whispers memory.

Though he lead you to the desert
or over hills where famine
flowers, like the locust
he devours what he loves most.

Saving none for tomorrow, or dawn
comes with empty arms, and he knows no way
to feed himself, feeding off others,
he has many, who find him, help him

you be one and dedicate your life
and misery to the upkeep of this cheapskate
you love so much no one else
seems to bridge the gap

with their common habits and rude manners,
his never were, a perfect gentleman
who leaves no trace, but lingers through the room
after he has gone, so I would follow

anywhere, over desert or mountain,
it's all the same if he's by my side.
The guide and wizard I would worship and obey,
my guardian teacher, who knows how to stay

alive on practically nothing in the city
until help comes, usually from a stranger or youth.
Such I am or was who knew no better
but all that I better forget now since I met you

and fell into that pit of the past with no escape.
You knock on the door, and off I go with you
into the night with not even a cent in my pockets,
without caring where or when I get back

But if once you put your hand on my shoulders
as David Rattray did last evening
that would be enough, on the seventh night
of the seventh moon, when Herd Boy

meets the Weaving Lady in heaven
and wanders forever lost in arms
until dawn when you come no more.

Bet'

If love be dark, a confusion in the mind
Then let me go, compelled and blind
Over the highway to your place where
Love is kind.

Hillside

Light songs play from phonograph
of a Viennese actress :
Perhaps by dawn we will forget

night held such memories of
beach house, sand, sun in trees.
Now seems enough to surrender

the tragic loss of each other,
let waves wash over that
fact we meet no more

on empire towers, burning pavilions
of desire. This fire holds
no emptier hands,

past triumphs present
midnights may do without.
We reached an ultimate shore,

if one travelled south,
your shadow went before.
By north, your star glowed.

Where may one go that
does not reach you,
somehow the snow,

  the mountains, meadows
  reveal your name,
  daynight, daybright, the same

      breaks upon the ear
      as a ship upon barriers

F

Of sound. And

You nowhere found
in the presence we await.
So it goes. Light gone low,

Melancholy caught in throat.
Build your boat and carry it out

to sea melodies drownd in tide.

Where Fled

                Despair long given me
as others' daily bread. What wish past this?
of wry stuff fed. Does desperate birth
bring one re-incarnation?

                Night nurtures
trust in dawn. Let one scrap of light
disappear from afternoon, all
murmur : too soon/shadowed darkness falls.

Does doom come on? We continue
walking on. What walls. Fled by whom.
The moon's an easy answer
to shine through blood and clouds.

'I despair of love . . .'

I despair of love
  ever throwing up
    on these shores,
enough of a raft for me
  to ride upon
    out to sea.

Jive

Tomorrow some motel with a guy,
Who'd have thought my dreams would come to this?
It's better than junk.
At least in a clean bed.

Then movies with mother.
The cycle goes on.
It's two o'clock in the morning
Rain on street.

After all, this toughness only goes to state
I'm out for anything
And will settle for nothing less. A dollar bill
Blow in the wind.

Impasse

Is it enough my feet blackend
    from streets of the city?
My hands coarsend, lovely limbs
    bone to dust.

Is it enough? my heart hardend
arms thickend eyes dim.
Is it enough I lost sight of him
Ages ago and still follow after
    on some blind, dumb path?

Is this aftermath? Am I ever
to follow that, always
The same man, one dream
to death, only another
Dream one never wakes from.

Cities stretch eternal streets
lead on. Star-points of light
flicker over the harbor. Oceans
beckon. I cover the waterfront
who have been near no docks.

They are too lonely.
There is no audience watching there
through the night
to reflect one's own face
passing in a glass.

It is eternal audience
and my feet hardend, my heart
blackend, nodding and
bowing before it.

Joy

burst in on us : a rare blossom.
Joie; a french word for happiness
that's just a thing called Joe.

Do you know him? He lives across
the border in provinces of grass.

Promise you tell him
I asked for him; you take me

To see him someday; a perfume
with his name on it

can be bought at Patou
for 12.50 $\frac{1}{8}$ of an ounce.

It comes in
a green leather case
with gold cap, stitched up one side

his name
hollow letters of gold.

Night Samba

My mother sleeps in her bed,
a figure of the forgotten past

Priests asleep in Chestnut Hill
dream of lascivious young infantas.

Their dreams a shattered
Grenoble landscape.

When will I ever cross your mists,
saffron in the dawn?

Clouds hang over the mountain
It's such a long way
to attain the joys of yesterday.

Gone wild living begets mere sorrow.
When will I ever catch up with

that saxophone, Stan
Getz, you pestilence.

Hypnagogic

By banks of the Neponset River
lies our house.
At night I hear voices of Indian spirits
call out to me:
'Each year these waters claim a pale face.'

I remember as children
how we built a hut to sit inside
hands touching in the dark,
how we sailed downstream on a raft
until Mother came through the woods
with a switch.
I remember an old well covered up with boards
and leaves, brown
from fallen trees,
birch and oak.

Winter now
boys skate on thin ice
by railroad tracks
they built a fence
no more will we see
that old woman, redhead
who floated downstream
bloated from the current,
nor She coming through the woods
curses on her mouth, in a red coat,
making her way to us
who sail on foamy rapids.

Parking Lot

Don't give nothing for nothing,
yet I blew a guy today
for eight dollars.

He gave me nothing.
I paid him.
O sin that wreaks vengeance

on them lidden children of the world.
I stole the money from Steve Jonas,
'bread from a poet.'

Damned and cursed before all the world
That is what I want to be.

Berkeley St Bridge

Petrified the wood
wherein we walk.

Frozen the fields.

Cruising these empty city streets
gets you nowhere.

Will you ever be saved, John?
I doubt it.

This world's got nothing for me.

No gods, mother, boys, beauty

It's too easy, begs description.
Defies the gods. Leaves something out
We were listening to other voices
in the afternoon : children, birds, ghosts
of haunted silence. Trucks.

Bells play across Columbus Avenue
I don't know why. We were asleep
In our pain. Another order descended,

where transmitted to an enchanted plain
behind intellect there was reason
and we were not commanded by gods, too.

To Denise Levertov

1.

Is it really you come to me
        after all these years
    writing in darkness,
            only moon for light,
                head on my arms,
            hearing your feathers
    rustle   in flight
            these pages

2.

I hear you speak in the night
voice across miles.
Shall I turn on the light
to destroy this moment?

Tones of your voice fill shadows in that darkness
myself at your fountain,
beside me in the room.
Believe me, when I say it's enough.

No other in this world but you.
No therefore, or thereafter.
Your voice falls silent, when I listen,
When I pick up a pen to write, gone completely.

The Old Man:

All about the sexual urge strikes in the night,
lover moves to beloved, mouth closes upon mouth.
Nowhere do the lonely stand long, unattended.
In dark rooms, cocks bulge against trousers.
A dull image, to the sexually uninitiated.

But to me now, came memories of what men call lust,
that excuse allowed them to press up together moments.
Call it desire. No, more than that. In need
Of oblivion from time, to possess and be possessed.
I know no other cause. Loneliness calls through the house

like a curse, but falls on deaf ears. Locked here
blind by poverty, my disease to seek out on some dark
   highway
That lover who will release me into heaven. Dim respite
which ends when his arms let me go. If even that. No arms
exist for me, but those locked in doors.
In other arms, in love with me, but still sharing
Other arms for ecstasy.

                              Holy saturday

94

On Sunday . . .

listening with you.
On Sunday—
to old poems.

The mood hits us,
moves us on—
a higher plane.

Sunday
when I'm with you
All day long.

Lordy, isn't this a swell Sunday,

listening here with you.

'Some black man looms in my life . . .'

Some black man looms in my life, larger than life.
Some white man hovers there too, but I am through with
   him.
Some wild man dreams through my day, smeiling of
   heroin.
Some dead man dies in my arms every night.

To H.

I like Sunday evenings after you're here.
I use your perfume to pretend you're near
in the night. My eyes are bright, why
can't I have a man of my own?

Your wife's necklace's around my neck
and even though I do shave I pretend
I'm a woman for you
you make love to me like a man.

Even though I hear you say why man
he doesn't even have any teeth
when I take out my plate
I make it up to you in other ways.

I will write this poem.

The Eagle Bar

A lamp lit in the corner
the Chinese girl talks to her lover
At bar, saxophone blares—

blue music, while boy in white turtleneck
    sweater
seduces the polka player from Poland
left over from Union party.

Janet sits beside me,
Barbra Streisand sings on Juke box
James tends bar

It's the same old scene
In Buffalo or Boston
yen goes on, continues in glare

of night, searching for its bait
oh will we go
where will we search

between potato chips and boys,
for impeccable one
that impossible spy

who does not come
with fresh air and sea
off Lake Erie

but stays home, hidden in sheets
with his wife and child alone
ah, the awful ache

as cash register rings
James the bartender sweeps
bottles off the bar.

Our Unborn Child

A butterfly inside you died
in my dream. It had orange wings.

L'Invitation au Voyage II

Look how rain fallen through the night
leaves woods hot, moist and calm,
how bird skims across grass
with no car in sight, awaiting return.

This that promised land *au bout du monde*
where humid winds blow against your ankles,
dragon lilies on fences open to the sun
Baudelaire's song heard again afternoon's vagabond.

Your lips an history of the heart
your hands hot deserts on my brow
your eyes grey mirrors I would drown
for if to die would do it now

this kiss in my mouth,
your words the vow.

My dear girl, I know no way
to go on loving you
but this one. Our lives entwined
as a huntsman's bow.

Oh archer, skill my hands
land this arrow close to bounds

that we cleave as wings on air
before transparent stranger appears
to take her away
in form of death or love

I'll take her away with me somewhere.

'Beauty never as mine . . .'

Beauty never as mine
Existed here for a day with you

If I loved you less
should you love me more,
or if I cared for you
would you not care for me?

What foolish questions to ask
two who are in love
as if answer prove
what one already knew.

We do not live, nor shall
we die, whose destinies
entwine, extant as a star
caring more for you by far.

The Legends

Moving like a dream like Ibeza
through midnight cities of the world
buying dreams of men and their hearts
to adorn dressing room tables, how many ornaments
to wear for dinner, or at selfish supper parties

this sale does not show by candlelight, their children
unheard stray in the night, odd pregnancies
abortions uncounted, smashed faces
wrenched hearts left behind at harborside
with ships pulled out.

I speak of suicides, men dropped to tide
sleeping pills that still our aching mind
lovers murdered because they are too kind,
anything to remain beautiful must stay blind
to those men turned past swine.

Ina O'Shea

used a shillealagh.
She worshipped stars
deep in the heart of Texas.
The moon above the man,
I love boop boop a doo
deep in the heart of Texas.

Lady be good. Redeem that other
horror.   Hour.   Sands in the glass
of ocean. Wiggle it around willya
down beneath the border
men seem lonesome locked
in their cells of service.

Leave them out willya
cries Ina O'Shea deep
in the heart of conscience.

Water and wood, be good
if you could, beguile
if you can, without it
you plan any old man
in the mood will do,
cries Ina O'Shea who

in her lonely room's blue
from the window of plenty.
Help yourself to another bowl

cries the unholy howl
of wolves in Texas.
We keep light deep
by the night of

juicy bosoms stuped
in oil from her heart's harvest.

Autumnal Ina O'Shea
creaking springs of stone.
Song let me in the world.

What Happened?

Better than a closet martinet.
      Better than a locket
        in a lozenge.
     At the market, try and top it
            in the Ritz.

Better than a marmoset
      at the Grossets,
   better than a mussel
       in your pockets.
        Better than a faucet
        for your locker,
        better not
     clock it.
    Better than a sachet
     in your cloche,
         better than a hatchet
         in Massachusetts,
        Ponkapog.
      Pudget
    Sound
  lost and found.

Better than an asprin—
      apertif does it.
Better not ask
    how you caught it
      what has happened to me?

Better not lack it—
    or packet in at the Rickenbackers.
     Better tack it back
    in a basket
    for Davy Crockett

Better not stack it.
　Better stash it
　　　　　　on the moon.

　　　　　Oh Pomagranate
　　　　　　ah Pawtucket.

　　　　　Oh Winsocki or
　　　　　　Naragansett.

　　　Better not claque it. Better cash it in
　　　　　at Hackensack.
　　　　　Better not lock it
　　　　　　up again.

Ally

My father's black ashtray
hollowed out of 1930 foes
of woe and death

he let me have at home, on
choking highways of disease through
Canton Avenue, Brush Hill Road

Blue Hills Parkway. Bought anew
in 1932? it stands here still
to fill the sad stuffed cigarettes

of Philip Morris, Ltd.

Elizabeth

By tenement window and lovers' room
abandoned notes from another time
chase leaves and acorn born
on April wind.

By beaches of adolescence where we swam
a wanted woman burned in dream
from death uncovers faces
in the sand.

Weir

Scollay Square
should've stayed
there with Dillinger
's harlots and squares.

All-night Rialto Theatre
no cloister neither
was Jack's tattoo parlor
or The Crawford House Bar.

Casino Burlesque; rubber-tired
that after hrs. joint on Hanover
Street, leading to Haymarket-Lechmere
No. Station trains bound for Gloucester,

Jack Hammond's Castle & Fort Square.

Without direction outré architecture
repairs slums of dereliction, or were
they, huddled in doorways at dawn, loving one another by milk, bottles, papers

at the Red Top Inn, Hayes Bick diner?
What confusion and violence stare here
in Buffalo, a solemn peace appeared divine
there those mannered streets of despair.

Diesjelolon

DIES JIE LO LON
DIES IRON ROWS
A BOAT MORELY UPSTREAMS
LO LONE NOW
IONE SNOW YESTERDAYS SE STER
DO ROW ME
UPSTREAM NOW
THITS ALL IO ASK FOR YOU
NOWE TEN YEARS OLDEN
THAN YOU NO JOSPREY

from *Nerves*
With Meaning

Rise, shining martyrs
over the multitudes
for the season of migration
between earth and heaven.

Rise shining martyrs
cut down in fire
and darkness,
speeding past light
straight through imagination's park.

In the smart lofts on West Newton St.
or the warehouse district of S.F., come,
let us go back
to bequeathed memory

of Columbus Ave., or the beach
at the end of Polk St.,
where Jack Spicer went,
or Steve Jonas' apts.
all over town

from Beacon Hill to St. Charles,
without warning how they went.
The multitude of martyrs,
staring out of

town houses now on Delaware Ave.
in the grey mist
of traffic circles, taking LSD
then not holding up
to rooming houses, Berkeley and motorcycles.

Books of poems all we had
to bound the frustration
of leaving them behind
in Millbrook mornings, on the swing

with Tambimuttu, exercising his solar plexus
during conversation. Each street
contains its own time of
other decades, recollected
after the festival, carefully

as so many jewels
to brush aside for
present occupation.
A printing press by the Pacific,

a Norman cottage in the east,
dancing to Donovan, in Pucci pajamas,
or perhaps prison, past imagination's plain,
with Saturday night sessions in the tombs, oh yes
rise shining martyrs, out of the movie house's matinee

on Long Island, to your love walking by
in the sun. Over the multitudes,
shortripping. And backyard swimming pools
of Arizona or Pacific Palisades,

in the canyons of L.A.
plus the journeys over oceans
and islands, to metropolis
spreadeagled the earth.
Yes rise shining martyrs

out of your graves, tell us
what to do, read your poems
under springtime moonlight.
Rise and salvage our century.

The Suck

This morning
last evening, yes
terday afternoon

      in the hall
your voice, full
of compliment

turns to strike
someone you do not

know as a wife or brother,

shaking, trembling
in your arms
sweating like seventeen

again under young middle-aged

bellies in the summer.

Insulted

I never rewarded, never cared
why didn't I
when they burnt your head

saw you beat mother instead
after you're dead
suspended

in what you shouldn't
despite one-eyed poison
from the woodshed

had to look upward
or under black polished stove
his dreaded tread,

marks of the rapist,
fed teacher coal shovel
flames of hatred

in bed that noon
heard shredded thread
of parentage divided.

Not David, was it?
no it isn't, heavy handed
she said, derided

what I didn't hear,
that spring Czecho-
slovakian spread folded,

bled all over the floor included
I fled for the door,
who needs that old maid

I didn't care, I wouldn't

Naked

An old man and a woman
came to torment me
in the desert with ants
and honey.

Three children set me free
marching proudly over the
clearing, tearing bands
of meat

from my arms, leaving
me empty to meet my love.
Who was waiting in bed
for me.

Piazza

throw keys down
to a man in the square
reading papers by sunlight

well-built, immune to flattery
who holds his own so long
outside the park

forbidden entrance, no matter
how often he slides
denied quiet interruption, the strength

of single gesture lost
twin alloy to true counsel
man's fault returns original habit.

Desperation

In what mad pursuit, or competition
the marvelous denies object
to what subject melancholy resignation?

drowned exile flight
down what exit, fall's fused endeavor
discharges incessant order

for what crushed languor,
what hapless ascension
rejected entreaties pace

cruel chase, within vain decline?
Annoyed, over-drawn, exempt
to what rest, borrowed dichotomy

unmasks its single purpose. ·

Acceptance

Should I wear a shadowed eye,
      grow moustaches
      delineate my chin

accept spit as offering
      attach a silver earring
      grease my hair

give orders to legions
      of lovers to maintain manhood
      scimitars away as souvenirs?

Sooush, beloved! here is my tongue.

Consolation

Waiting at the window
in winter
for some trace of spring?

or any figure
to ease incoherent
blindness from absence

There's one tree out there
with still a patch of snow
on its trunk

and a cat in the yard
though birds are missing
for days due to storm.

It's best not to think too much.
What awaits but death?
A long life of misery.

As branches bend in wind
we accept this futility
looking for love

Knowing we never will find same.
What to do but grow
away from the sun

Unless to think on the past
a vapor that escapes
from the mind in impatience.

Best to get away from one's self
one's own life
for it leads to frustration

no matter who one is,
or what he has done.
The loneliness of hotels linger

in grey mid-Manhattan
in mid-morning mist
as taxis splash through rain.

Feminine Soliloquy

If my dreams were lost in time
as books and clothes,
my mind also went down the line
and infused with other longing

of a desperate sort, a sexual kind
of nightmare developed where every breath was
aimed at another man, who did not know
it, until I informed him by letter

And said nothing. As delusions lift off
I see I paid an ultimate price
and left in loneliness, nervous shaking
wracks day and night with residue.

It's impossible to make clear.
I wanted something, someone
I could not have, until I began
to sound like him, imitate him

at his shy insistence from a distance.
A Venice where floods of onanism took hold.
This self-indulgence has not left me.
Normal relations seem mild.

I am drowsy and half-awake to the world
from which all things flow.
I see it as growing old
if only the price paid were not so great,

And what I wanted wanted me.
But it cannot be.
I wished these things since I was twelve
and the more impossible, or resistant

to the need, the deeper hold they had on me.

Reading in Bed

by evening light, at the window, where wind blows
it's not enough to wake with morning
as a child, the insistent urge of habit

sound, to write a poem, to pore over one's past
recall ultimate orders one has since doubted
in despair. Inner reality returns

of moonlight over water at Gloucester, as
fine a harbor as the Adriatic, Charles said, before the big storm
blew up to land ancient mooring, shard against sand

of memory at midnight; ah yes the dream begins
of lips pressed against yours over waves, tides,
hour-long auto rides into dawn, when time

pounds a mystery on the beach, to no death out of reach.

Stop Watch

the sensation
1) of 10 assorted dancers
   in a crowded dining room

   moving as one person
2) in unison
   to a popular tune

   during late afternoon
3) hip and thighs beat
   with sparkling feet

   over the stucco floor
4) before an open door
   how fortunate, how poor

   we were without the sign,
5) symbol of recurrence
   or occurrence

   surrounded
6) by buff walls
   it was not a waltz

   only a standard rock
7) song, much as students
   speak in rejoinder

   to a classroom; the same decibels
8) happened in a bookstore when I rose
   using the newspaper I had as a fan;

   the leaves of clover
9) fluttering these three
   unities I have known

as a tone to a bell's
10) gong, none of them
lasting longer

than 10-12 seconds
11) pressing history, light
in memory reckoned.

Removed Place

When the echo falls
one will dismiss it.
When it calls again,
one will miss
it, falling in love with the present,
while one is able of it.
When the shadows enlarge, will one
enter it, or stay where
he is now. What will one do, how